Jesus Gets Hand-Me-Downs

J. Chris Richards
Illustrated by Virginia J. Hanners

ILLUMIFY
MEDIA.COM

Introduction

Star light, Star bright, a special child is born this night.

On this night, Jesus was born in the small town of Bethlehem. An angel told the nearby shepherds about this special baby. After the shepherds visited the infant, they told their families about Him.

The wives decided since the young family did not have close relations in Bethlehem, they would bring gifts of food and items necessary to care for the Baby. The children of the shepherds also wanted to bring gifts but did not have money to purchase presents.

So, they gathered things they no longer needed or could find in the surrounding countryside.

Once they arrived at the stable, these children handed the gifts down to the baby and told Him the stories that surrounded these objects.

On the pages of this coloring book are pictures depicting the stories. Ask your parents to tell or read to you the stories depicted.

We hope you enjoy this coloring book and learn the stories at the same time.

All the stories can be found in the *Jesus Gets Hand-Me-Downs* book available at Amazon.com and BarnesandNoble.com.

The coloring pages are all on a right-hand page to avoid markers bleeding onto other pages. It's best to put a sheet of paper between pages as you color.

Blessings to each of you,

Chris and Virginia

Telling the story

A special basket to save a life

Who can catch whom

They would not bow to an idol

Shepherds in the wilderness for forty years

God is our special protector

A special robe to serve God

A pile of rocks to remember

Saving the Spies

Rebuilding the Walls

Choosing a staff

Animals two by two

How did the money get here

A jug for water

What can you do with sticks

Going Home

Jesus Gets Hand-Me-Downs

Published by
Illumify Media Global
www.IllumifyMedia.com
"Let's bring your book to life!"

Paperback ISBN: 978-1-964251-86-8

Cover design by Debbie Lewis

Printed in the United States of America